VICTOR HERBERT
ALBUM

37 Songs and Piano Pieces,

1895–1913

DOVER PUBLICATIONS, INC.

New York

Acknowledgments

The publisher is grateful to Sandy Marrone for lending the original sheet music of "Because You're You!" and "Dagger Dance," and to David A. Jasen and Donald Stubblebine for lending "Badinage," "Dance of the Marionettes" and "Jeannette and Her Little Wooden Shoes."

The following nine items were loaned by the ARCHIVE OF POPULAR AMERICAN MUSIC, UCLA (Victor T. Cardell, Head), which has once again significantly helped to make a Dover song album possible: "Al Fresco," "Angelus," "Every Lover Must Meet His Fate," "Go to Sleep, Slumber Deep!," "Pretty as a Picture," "Rose of the World," "Star Light, Star Bright," "Tramp! Tramp! Tramp!" and "When You're Pretty and the World Is Fair."

Published in Canada by General Publishing Company, Ltd., 30 Lesmill Road, Don Mills, Toronto, Ontario.

Published in the United Kingdom by Constable and Company, Ltd., 10 Orange Street, London WC2H 7EG.

Victor Herbert Album: 37 Songs and Piano Pieces, 1895-1913 is a new work, first published by Dover Publications, Inc., in 1990. It consists of unabridged, unaltered republications of the sheet music of 37 popular songs and piano pieces (original publishers and dates of publication are indicated in the Contents) and a new Introduction by Stanley Appelbaum.

Manufactured in the United States of America
Dover Publications, Inc., 31 East 2nd Street, Mineola, N.Y. 11501

Library of Congress Cataloging-in-Publication Data

Herbert, Victor, 1859–1924.
  [Selections; arr.]
  Victor Herbert album.

  Principally songs from operettas with acc. arr. for piano.
  "Unabridged, unaltered republications of the sheet music"—T.p. verso.
  Contains Badinage (1895) (orchestral work, arrangement for piano); and excerpts from The wizard of the Nile (1895), The fortune teller (1898), Babes in toyland (1903), It happened in Nordland (1904), Miss Dolly Dollars (1905), Mlle. Modiste (1905), The red mill (1906), (The rose of) Algeria (1908–1909), Naughty Marietta (1910), Natoma. Dagger dance (1911) [arr. for piano], The enchantress (1911), and Sweethearts (1913).
  1. Songs with piano. 2. Musicals—Excerpts, Arranged. 3. Piano music, Arranged. I. Title.
  M3.1.H53D7 1990   89-755342
  ISBN 0-486-26186-7

Introduction

DIVERSITY AND MULTIDIRECTIONALITY were keynotes of Victor Herbert's phenomenal career. Born in Dublin in 1859, even as a young boy he imbibed both the lilting traditional tunes of his grandfather, Samuel Lover,[1] and formal classical music training in Germany, where he grew up. It was from Germany that he came to New York in 1886—already a composer, instructor and virtuoso cellist—to join the Metropolitan Opera orchestra.

The atmosphere of the American music world at the moment was propitious for all of Herbert's talents, past and future. In an expansionist economy, industrial and financial magnates were lavishly patronizing classical music (the Boston Symphony Orchestra was founded in 1881, the Met in 1883). Blending swiftly and effortlessly into this cosmopolitan scene, Herbert performed, taught, and also composed strong and elegant works that were influential at the time and are still being recorded today. The pinnacle of his classical music career was his conductorship of the fledgling Pittsburgh Symphony Orchestra from 1898 to 1904. During his tenure he inculcated the highest standards of musicianship.

In another area of American music, the military band was enjoying immense popularity, John Philip Sousa and the older Patrick Sarsfield Gilmore being the preeminent bandmasters. When Gilmore died, Herbert, despite all other obligations, took over his band, remaining its leader from 1893 to 1900.

It is with the third aspect of Herbert's musical activities that this volume is chiefly concerned: his contribution to the American musical theater, which occupied most of his last thirty years, and with which he reached his broadest and most responsive public. Once again, the timing was right. Through an interlocking set of circumstances—availability of talent; transformation of the entertainment world into a huge industry characterized by "syndicates" and "circuits"; the coming of age of the sheet-music business; and the dissemination of songs and skits on disks and cylinders—America was on the verge of independence in this field, freeing itself from the stranglehold of Paris, Vienna and especially London. Herbert, though heavily influenced by his varied European heritage, was one of the men who helped create musical stage works that were specifically and unmistakably American.[2]

Even within the area of popular stage works, there was a marked dichotomy between the more classically tinged operettas, which often demanded highly trained voices (for instance, the two original leads of *Naughty Marietta*, Emma Trentini and Orville Harrold, sang with major opera companies, and Herbert wrote four operettas for the Met soprano Fritzi Scheff) and the more Tin Pan Alley–like shows dominated by popular comedians who were totally innocent of bel canto. Furthermore, some highly successful Herbert offerings, such as *The Red Mill*, were hybrids, containing elements of both the operatic and the clown types.

Delving into this realm of musical theater, the present anthology, with its 37 pieces ranging from 1895 through 1913, is probably the largest ever published. These are the most popular and well-remembered items, as indicated by their inclusion in published popularity listings and in old and new recordings of show excerpts; their appearance in films, radio and television; and the less tangible but no less real fact of their general recognition, their firm place in the public consciousness or subconscious. Naturally, over the years adaptations and alterations have sometimes crept in; the original sheet music reprinted here contains the pristine form of these treasures.[3]

"Badinage," a perennial "pops" item, possibly composed

---

[1]Tunes, phrases and grace notes with Irish associations are liberally sprinkled through Herbert's songs (think of the phrases "You are ever happy then" in "Toyland" and "the little darlings!" in "Every Day Is Ladies' Day with Me") even when the subject is not specifically Irish. (Only the show *Eileen* of 1917 had a thoroughly Irish milieu.)

[2]The brief sketch above merely indicates the enormous range of Herbert's strictly musical activities. There is no space here to portray the socialite, gourmet and bon vivant, or the champion of composers' rights who influenced the copyright law of 1909 and helped create ASCAP in 1913. (The standard biography is *Victor Herbert: A Life in Music*, by Edward N. Waters, 1955.)

[3]To hear the original tempos, rhythms and moods of some of these pieces, consult the three-LP album *The Early Victor Herbert: From the Gay Nineties to the First World War* (Smithsonian Institution/RCA, 1979). The "Early" is a misnomer, because the album reaches into the composer's peak period and covers all but his last eleven years. It has the same time range as the present anthology and even includes some original cast members of *The Fortune Teller* and *Sweethearts*.

as early as 1893, is one of the four instrumental pieces included here. Another, "Al Fresco"—cut from the same cloth as "Badinage"—was composed independently in 1904 but then added as an intermezzo in 1905 to an already running show, *It Happened in Nordland*. By contrast, both "The March of the Toys" from *Babes in Toyland* (1903) and "Dagger Dance" from the grand opera *Natoma* (1911) were not only integral but even climactic plot-developing numbers in their respective productions—examples of a born symphonist's dramatic thinking.[4]

"Star Light, Star Bright," from the second of Herbert's 40-odd shows (*The Wizard of the Nile*, 1895, starring comedian Frank Daniels), is one of the composer's numerous waltzes, but nevertheless basically a comic song, as indicated by the extra printed verses (the Jim Corbett–Bob Fitzsimmons fight referred to in verse 3 did actually take place in 1897). The musical phrase to which the words "Does the girl that I adore,/Love me less or love me more?" are sung is a direct reminiscence of a phrase in the opening chorus of Sullivan's *Iolanthe* (1882): "Arm ourselves with lovers' darts,/Hide ourselves in lovers' hearts."

The Fortune Teller (1898) was Herbert's most successful show score up to that point. "Gypsy Love Song" is one of his best-loved creations, and "Romany Life" is an impressive slow–fast *csárdás* (of the type immortalized by "Klänge der Heimat" in *Die Fledermaus*), its strong Magyar flavoring even including the Hungarian exclamation "Eljen!" ("Long live . . . !").

Babes in Toyland (1903) was a Chicago-originated extravaganza meant to cash in on the immense success of a 1902 Chicago production, *The Wizard of Oz*. Whereas the potpourri *Wizard* score was jejune, however, Herbert endowed his own *Babes* with a wealth of memorable music.

It Happened in Nordland (1904), antedating *Call Me Madam* by 46 years as a show about a perky American ambassadress to a fictional European country, had three different female leads in its two-season New York run. This was due to the displeasure of Herbert, who would not allow his stars to interpolate material by other composers. Though his attitude caused him anguish at the moment, he was striking a blow for musical integrity on the popular stage at a time when this privilege was normally vouchsafed only to such venerated (and dead) masters as Offenbach, Strauss and Sullivan.

Miss Dolly Dollars (September 1905) was a vehicle for the popular singing actress Lulu Glaser. The title of "A Good Cigar Is a Smoke" is a quotation from Kipling's poem "The Betrothed."

Mlle. Modiste (December 1905) was a box-office smash. Its most famous number, the "dreamy sensuous waltz" "Kiss Me Again," comes at the end of the scena "If I Were

on the Stage," a gamut-of-the-moods routine clearly inspired by "Spiel' ich die Unschuld vom Lande," the third-act aria of the stagestruck chambermaid Adele in *Die Fledermaus*.

The Red Mill (1906) was an audience-winning amalgam of high jinks (the stars were Montgomery and Stone, whose *Wizard of Oz* Herbert had set out to surpass with *Babes in Toyland*) and traditional operetta, with one "serious" young couple and one comic older couple—all with appropriate numbers of no great technical difficulty. Montgomery and Stone played brash Americans in Europe (like the title character of Cohan's 1904 *Little Johnny Jones*), and their popular number "The Streets of New York"—a paean to the metropolis by temporary exiles—was the equivalent of that show's "Give My Regards to Broadway."

Algeria of 1908 resurfaced as *The Rose of Algeria* in 1909. Of the six scores that Herbert crammed into the four years between *The Red Mill* and *Naughty Marietta*, it was the least ephemeral and most tuneful.

Naughty Marietta (1910) is surely Herbert's masterpiece. The number of melodious and inventive songs is astonishing. "Tramp! Tramp! Tramp!" seems to have set the pattern for catchy marches sung by paramilitary male leads; its spirit is echoed in the Mounties' song in *Rose Marie* (Friml, 1924), the "Song of the Riffs" in *The Desert Song* (Romberg, 1926) and "Stout-Hearted Men" in *The New Moon* (Romberg, 1928), to mention just a few instances. This show may also contain the best bunch of lyrics that Herbert ever set, even though his authors were generally among the best of the day.

Doubtless the worst text Herbert had to contend with was the libretto of his first grand opera, *Natoma* (February 1911; fortunately, only its most popular instrumental number is reprinted here). Herbert's second grand opera, *Madeleine*, was produced at the Met in 1913. Neither work has maintained itself in the repertoire.

Plans for a second operetta with Emma Trentini, the original Marietta, collapsed when she flitted to the camp of the young Rudolf Friml, starring in his *Firefly* in 1912. Herbert's best effort between *Naughty Marietta* and *Sweethearts* was *The Enchantress* (October 1911), with the English operetta singer Kitty Gordon. (The number of Herbert operetta characters who either were or wanted to be prima donnas was legion!—see the *Enchantress* song included here and the list of other songs on the show cover, reproduced on page 143.)

The present volume ends fittingly with selections from one of Herbert's most delightful scores. *Sweethearts* (1913), starring Christie MacDonald, was a lyrical Ruritanian romance. During the preceding six years, America had been gaining familiarity with the lusty and vigorous melodies of the newer Viennese operetta school—Lehár, Oscar Straus, Kálmán—and the title waltz of *Sweethearts* is just such a broadly conceived, muscular tune—one of the greatest waltzes ever composed in America.

---

[4]Dover hopes to reprint another major instrumental piece, "Indian Summer" (1919)—as well as the dozen or so great songs Herbert wrote between 1913 and his death in 1924—in future anthologies.

Contents

The sequence is basically chronological, by year of original performance or publication. Within the grouping for each stage production, the songs are in alphabetical order, using their titles as printed on the first page of music, and not counting an opening "A" or "The." Each individual show had a standard song-sheet cover design for all its songs, which is reproduced once only in each case.

Alphabetical List of Songs, Piano Pieces and Shows

Alternate song titles are included. Show titles are in italics. Opening words "A" and "The" are not counted.

Badinage.

by

Victor Herbert.

2

Badinage

You come home at night and your wife's smile is bright,
  She will give you a loving kiss.
You sit down to dine and the dinner is fine;
  'Tis a case of domestic bliss.
She brings you your slippers, your best cigars;
  With affection she holds your hand.
She sits on your knee, she is sweet as can be,
  But why you cannot understand.

        Star light – Star bright
          Very first star I see to night
        Tell me, tell me, all I wish to know
          All this kindness is too much.
        This must be a case of "touch."
          Star light–Star bright.
        Tell me is it so?

3.

In the papers we've seen all the news there has been
  Of a certain prospective fight.
They've flooded the nation with rash conversation
  Till the public is wearied quite.
They travelled as "stars"; They've quarrelled in bars;
  They tried each other's noses to pull;
But when they take hold they'll find I am told
  That they both have their hands pretty full.

        Star light – Star bright
          Very first star I see to night
        Tell me, tell me, all I wish to know
          If ever they do put on the mitts,
        Will "Fitz" have "Jim", or "Jim" have Fitz?
          Star light – Star bright.
        Tell me is it so?

Star light, star bright.

Words by HARRY B. SMITH.

Music by
VICTOR HERBERT.

jealous-y mocks and teas-es you Of some-one that's far a-way,_ To the

first star that peers, just con-fide all your fears, And this lit-tle for-mu-la

Tempo di Valse.

rit. *pp mezzo voce.*

a tempo.

rit. *pp*

say:_ Star light, star

bright Ver-y first star I see to night,

Tell me: is it so?

VOCAL SELECTIONS
FROM
THE FORTUNE TELLER
COMIC OPERA IN 3 ACTS.

BOOK BY **HARRY B. SMITH.** MUSIC BY **VICTOR HERBERT.**

Under the direction of
Milton and Sargent Aborn

Always do as People say You should.

SONG & REFRAIN.

50

M · WITMARK · & · SONS
NEW YORK   CHICAGO   LONDON   SAN FRANCISCO.
JOSEF WEINBERGER, LEIPZIG AND VIENNA
ALLAN & CO., MELBOURNE, AUSTRALIA
CANADIAN-AMERICAN MUSIC CO. LTD., TORONTO

ALWAYS DO AS PEOPLE SAY YOU SHOULD.

Words by Harry B. Smith.

Music by Victor Herbert.

My a-ged grand-ma told me And I've
And now I am a grown up girl I'm

read the same in books That it
still as good as pie And I

doesn't mat-ter what a girl may
do as peo-ple tell me or at

wear or how she looks. She nev-er should be friv-o-lous; She
least I al-ways try; For in-stance with an of-fi-cer, a

nev - er should be bold. My grand-ma said:"My dar-ling al-ways
hand-some young dra-goon I went out for an ev'-ning walk, a

do as you are told." When grand-ma said:"Don't touch the jam," I
stroll by light of moon. I blush to say he kissed me It was

mind-ed her re-quest. I did not care a bit for jam. I
ver-y rude and bold. But he told me not to scream and so I

liked the jel - ly best "Be punct - u - al at meals," she said, "or
did as I was told He told me then to kiss him It was

I shall have to scold" And I was al - ways there you see I
ver - y im - pu - dent But I tho't what grand-ma told me and I

did as I was told.
was o - be - di - ent.

Moderato con sentimento.

Al - ways do as peo - ple say you should, You
Al - ways do as peo - ple say you should, You

GYPSY LOVE SONG.

(Slumber on, my little gypsy sweetheart.)

Words by Harry B. Smith.

Music by Victor Herbert.

Baritone and Mezzo Bass in A.

1. The birds of the for - est are call-ing for thee___ And the
2. The fawn that you tamed has a look in its eyes___ That doth

shades and the glades___ are lone - ly; ___ Summer is there with her blos - soms
say "We are too___ long part - ed;" ___ Songs that are trolled by our com - rades

fair, ___ And you are ab - sent on - ly. ___ No
old ___ Are not now as they were ___ light heart - ed. ___ The

Romany Life.
(Song a là Czardas.)

Words by HARRY B.SMITH.

Music by VICTOR HERBERT.

poco rit

We have a home 'neath the for-est shades, Nev-er an-y oth-er have

we. _____ Nev-er an-y oth-er have we. _____ Our

a tempo

camp - fires glow in the nooks and glades, Where our tents are white _____ to

see. _____ Where our tents are white __ to see. ___

Wand'ring ev-er__ here _____ and there. _____ Our roof _____ is the

sky a-bove__ Ju-che! __ but the Rom-an-y eyes__ are rare, __ And the

molto rit e dim.

Rom-an-y life _____ is__ love. _____

none   can be   Half   so   mer - ry _____ as lads of

Rom - an - y.   None   so   gay   as   we, The lads of Rom - an - y,

None   so   gay   as   we, the lads of Rom - an - y.   El - jen! _____

_____ El - jen! _____   Ha! _____

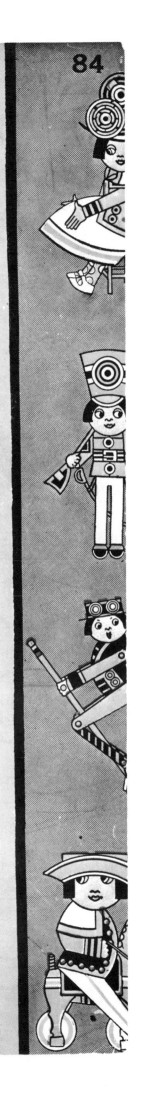

HAMLIN & MITCHELL'S
STUPENDOUS EXTRAVAGANZA AS PRODUCED
AT THE GRAND OPERA HOUSE, CHICAGO.

BABES IN TOYLAND

BOOK AND LYRICS BY
GLEN MacDONOUGH
MUSIC BY
VICTOR HERBERT

M. WITMARK & SONS
NEW YORK   CHICAGO   LONDON
VIENNA-LEIPZIG   SAN FRANCISCO

Go to Sleep, Slumber Deep!

LULLABY

Words by
GLEN MAC DONOUGH.

Music by
VICTOR HERBERT.

Fades the day a - way____
Close thy drow - sy eyes____

Night is com-ing dear____
Dark the shad-ows grow____

I Can't Do The Sum.

Jane and Piper Children.

Lyric by
GLEN MAC DONOUGH.

Music by
VICTOR HERBERT.

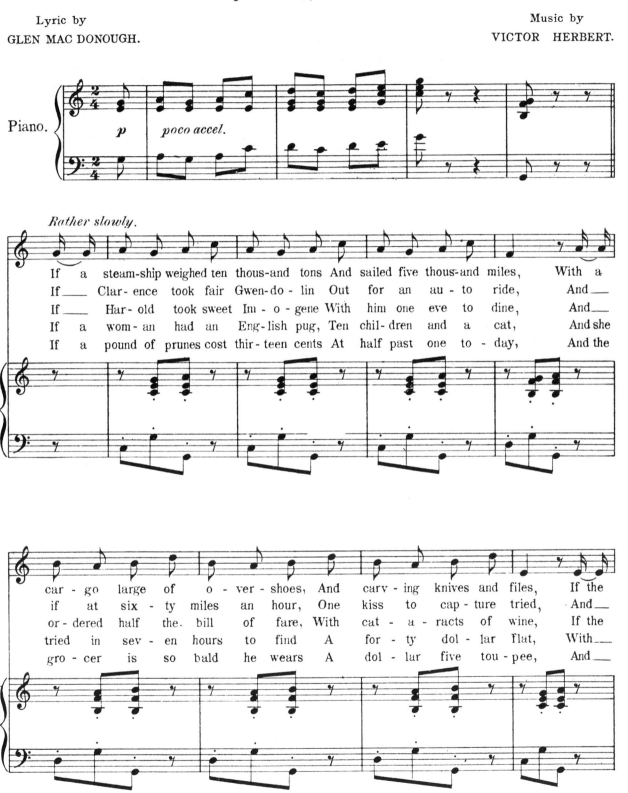

If a steam-ship weighed ten thous-and tons And sailed five thous-and miles, With a
If Clar - ence took fair Gwen-do - lin Out for an au - to ride, And
If Har - old took sweet Im - o - gene With him one eve to dine, And
If a wom-an had an Eng-lish pug, Ten chil-dren and a cat, And she
If a pound of prunes cost thir - teen cents At half past one to - day, And the

car - go large of o - ver - shoes, And carv - ing knives and files, If the
if at six - ty miles an hour, One kiss to cap - ture tried, And
or - dered half the bill of fare, With cat - a - racts of wine, If the
tried in sev - en hours to find A for - ty dol - lar flat, With
gro - cer is so bald he wears A dol - lar five tou - pee, And

THE CHILDREN.

March of the Toys

from

"Babes in Toyland."

by VICTOR HERBERT.

Molto moderato.

March of the Toys

Toyland.

Tom, Tom.

Lyric by
GLEN MAC DONOUGH.

Music by
VICTOR HERBERT.

Absinthe Frappè.

Prince George and Chorus.

Lyric by
GLEN MAC DONOUGH.

Music by
VICTOR HERBERT.

Allegro.

Molto moderato.

When   life   seems
The   deed   is

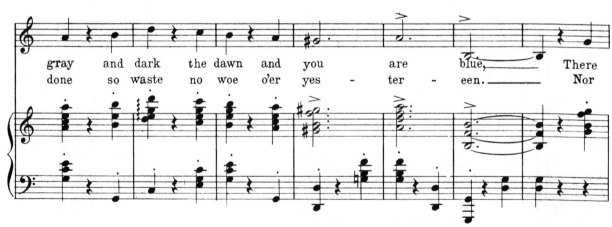

gray   and dark   the dawn and   you   are   blue,   There
done   so waste   no woe o'er   yes -   ter - een.   Nor

born of a night of the bowl, _____ Like a sun 'twill rise through the
in - ky skies That so heav-i-ly hang o'er your soul. _____ At the
first cool sip on your fe - vered lip You de - ter-mine to live through the
day, _____ Life's a - gain worth while as with dawn - ing smile You im-

bibe your ab - sinthe frap - pè.

SOP. & ALTO.

TEN.

BASS.

It will free you first from the

It will free you first from the

pp

burn - ing thirst That is born of a night of the bowl._____ Like a

burn - ing thirst That is born of a night of the bowl._____ Like a

accel. *rit.*

sun 'twill rise through the in - ky skies That so heav-i-ly hang o'er your

sun 'twill rise through the in - ky skies That so heav-i-ly hang o'er your

accel. *rit.*

"Al Fresco"

Intermezzo.

Allegretto giocoso.

VICTOR HERBERT.

LULU GLASER

IN CHARLES DILLINGHAM'S PRODUCTION OF

MISS DOLLY DOLLARS

MUSIC BY
VICTOR HERBERT

A MUSICAL COMEDY

LYRICS BY
HARRY B. SMITH

Otto Sarony Co.
N.Y.

M. WITMARK & SONS
NEW YORK · CHICAGO · LONDON · SAN FRANCISCO
BOTE · BOCK · BERLIN · LEIPZIG AND VIENNA
MELBOURNE, AUSTRALIA

EDGAR
FELLER

A Good Cigar Is A Smoke.

PUFF, PUFF, PUFF.

Words by
HARRY B. SMITH.

Music by
VICTOR HERBERT.

If a pair of blue eyes have de - ceived you, And a
When you find that your lat - est flir - ta - - tion Is be -

pair of red lips said you nay,_____ Don't ap -
com - ing too ser - i - ous quite,_____ And you're

peal to cham-pagne, All its bub-bles are vain, You will
get-ting too fond Of a bru-nette or blonde, Call a

on-ly feel worse the next day._____ Just for-
halt, lad, and set your-self right._____ Love per-

get for-tune's snub and drop in at the club Where you
haps ends in smoke, But its rings are no joke, They dis-

know all the good fel-lows are,_____ There the ton-ic you're aft-er is
solve not nor van-ish a - far;_____ They are put on to stay there, They

gos - sip and laugh - ter, You light up a long dark ci - gar.
won't float a - way there, Like rings you blow from your ci - gar.

Tempo di Valse.

Puff,   puff,   puff,   puff,   Watch - ing the

smoke 'a - ris - - ing;   Puff,   puff,

puff,   puff,   Soon you'll be re - a - liz - - ing

CHAS. DILLINGHAM'S PRODUCTION

OF

Mlle. Modiste

AS·SUNG
BY··THE
FRITZI
SCHEFF
COMIC
OPERA
COMPANY

MUSIC BY
VICTOR HERBERT

BOOK & LYRICS BY
HENRY BLOSSOM

M. WITMARK & SONS
NEW YORK · CHICAGO · LONDON · SAN FRANCISCO

If I Were On The Stage.

(Kiss Me Again.)

Fifi.

Lyric by
HENRY BLOSSOM.

Music by
VICTOR HERBERT.

I were asked to play the part, Of sim-ple maid-en light of heart, A vil-lage lass in coun-try clothes, As to and from her work she goes; I'd

Tra la, la, la, la, la, Tra la, la, la, la, Tra la, la, la, la,

Tra la, la, la, la, la, la, Tra la, la, la, la, la, la, la, Tra la, la, la, la, la, la, tra

Allegro.

la. ___

If

Meno mosso.

they should of - fer me some day, A pri - ma don - na role to play, A

state - ly queen with pow-dered hair, Her cost - ly gowns and jew - els rare; I

would not act the part a - miss, I'd sing a pol - o - naise like this.

Tempo di Polonaise. *con bravura.*

this. Ah, you will all a - gree that hap-py I should be, Ah!—

—— I'm queen of all the land. Ah!————— Ah!—————

I Want What I Want When I Want It.

Lyric by
HENRY BLOSSOM.

Music by
VICTOR HERBERT.

wife.____ I drink my fill if I have the will with
all.____ Of course, your life, if you have no wife, is

poco meno.

friends who are tried and old,____ And oft when the com-pa-ny's
lone-some at times and slow,____ But wheth-er you mar-ry or

a tempo.

good, I stay, I may not come home till the break of day, But if
not they say, You're bound to re-gret____ it ei-ther way; Let

accel.   *rit* ____   *molto marcato.*

din-ner is wait-ing and I am a-way, There is no one to nag me or
those who are sin-gle be sor-ry who may, I'd be sor-ri-er mar-ried I

self I de-ny, There's no one to ask me the
self I de-ny, There's no one to ask me the

where - fore or why, I eat when I'm hun-gry, and
where - fore or why, I eat when I'm hun-gry, and

drink when I'm dry. For I want what I want when I
drink when I'm dry. For I want what I want when I

want it! I want what I want when I want it!
want it! I want what I want when I want it!

DAVID MONTGOMERY AND FRED. A. STONE

IN CHARLES DILLINGHAM'S PRODUCTION

The RED MILL

BOOK & LYRICS BY

HENRY BLOSSOM

MUSIC BY

VICTOR HERBERT

SELECTION.....1.00   WALTZES.....75   MARCH.....50
LANCIERS.........50   SCORE.........2.00

Theatrical and Music Hall Rights of this Song are
Reserved. For permission apply to the Publishers.

M. WITMARK & SONS

NEW YORK   CHICAGO   LONDON   SAN FRANCISCO.   JOSEF WEINBERGER, LEIPZIG AND VIENNA   ALLAN & CO. MELBOURNE, AUSTRALIA   CANADIAN-AMERICAN MUSIC CO LTD. TORON

Because You're You!

Lyric by
HENRY BLOSSOM.

Music by
VICTOR HERBERT.

Molto moderato.

(Bertha.)
Love is a queer lit - tle el - fin sprite,

(Governor.)
Blest with the dead - li - est aim!

(Bertha.)
Shoot - ing his ar - rows to

left and right, Bag - ging the rar - est game.

Fill - ing our hearts with a glad sur - prise, Al - most too good to be true! And still can you tell me why do you love me? On - ly be - cause you are you, dear!

rit.

poco rit.

Refrain.

Not that you are fair, dear, Not that you are true.

Not that I am fair, dear, Not that I am

Slower

"Every Day Is Ladies' Day With Me"

Words by
HENRY BLOSSOM.

Music by
VICTOR HERBERT

"The Isle of our Dreams"

Doris and Gretchen.

Words by
HENRY BLOSSOM.

Music by
VICTOR HERBERT.

When my heart grows faint and wea-ry,——— when the

world goes sad-ly ill,——— It is sweet to hear you,

dea-rie ____ whisper that you love me still. _____ It is

sweet to talk with you, dear, ____ of the woods and crys - tal

streams, ____ and the ros - es wet with dew, dear, ____ in the

GRETCHEN.

is - land of our dreams. ____ In the beau-ti-ful isle of our

DORIS.

dreams, dear, there is nev-er a sor-row or pain, _____ Eve-ry

trou-ble and care quick-ly van-ish-es there and

all is made hap-py _____ a-gain. _____ So we'll

MOONBEAMS.

Lyric by
HENRY BLOSSOM.

Music by
VICTOR HERBERT.

The day is gone and the night comes on, And the birds have sought their nest,_____ The

The Streets of New York.

Con, Kid and Chorus.

Lyric by
HENRY BLOSSOM.

Music by.
VICTOR HERBERT.

In dear old New York it's re - mark - a - ble ver - y! The name on the lamp-post is un - nec - ess - ar - y! You
If a spare af - ter - noon you should hap - pen to have and you start on a lei - sur - ly stroll up Fifth Av - en - ue,
What - ev - er the weath - er is - shin - ing or show - er - y, That does-n't "cut an - y ice" on the Bow - er - y

mere - ly have to see the girls to know what
There is where with haugh - ty air you'll see them
Eve - ry night till broad day - light, they dance and

street you're on! Fifth Av - en - ue beau - ties and
as they walk! With vel - vets and lac - es and
sing and talk! The girls are all game and they're

sfz

dear old Broad - way girls! The tail - or - made shop - pers the
sab - les en - fold - ing them, real - ly you'll near - ly fall
jol - ly good fel - lows, They're not ver - y swell but they're

Av - en - ue "A" girls, They're strict-ly all right but they're dif - fer - ent
dead on be - hold - ing them, luck-y's the earl that can mar - ry a
none of them jeal - ous, They go it a - lone in a style of their

rit.   *piu rit.*

quite, In the diff - 'rent parts of town. _____ In
girl from Fifth Av - en - ue New York. _____
own On the Bow - ery in New York. _____

rit.   *piu rit.*

a tempo.

old New York! In old New York! The peach-crop's al - ways

a tempo.

94   The Streets of New York

fine! They're sweet and fair and on the square! The

maids of Man - hat-tan for mine! You can - not see in gay Pa -

ree, in Lon-don or in Cork! The queens you'll meet on

an - y street in old New York.

Dance.

When You're Pretty and the World is Fair.

ENSEMBLE.

From THE RED MILL.

Lyric by
HENRY BLOSSOM.

Music by
VICTOR HERBERT.

month of May   And old age is like De - cem - ber gray!_____   So we'll dance and sing and

play, we'll dance and sing and play, be hap-py while   we   may. _____

Dance.

Mʳ Frank McKee Presents The Musical Play

Algeria

Book and Lyrics by
Glen MacDonough

Music by
Victor Herbert

Chas. K. Harris
New York Chicago London.

Ask Her While The Band Is Playing.

Millicent and Female Chorus.

Lyric by
GLEN MAC DONOUGH.

Music by
VICTOR HERBERT.

Ask Her While the Band is Playing

Love is like a Cigarette.

De Lome and Male Chorus.

Lyric by
GLEN MAC DONOUGH.

Music by
VICTOR HERBERT.

Moderato grazioso.

DE LOME.

My ci - gar - ette, Sweet sol-ace bring to me Thy
My ci - gar - ette, Thou art a mag - ic key Un -

mys - tic mists Are filled with fan - tas - y, In thee I hold A
- to the lock That pris - ons mem - o - ry! A touch from thee Will

nec - ro - man - cers wand, From lead - en care 'Twill sev - er ev - 'ry bond, Thy
op - en wide the door, And ghosts re - lease Of days that are no more Be -

in-cense mounts___ In swirl-ing curves a-bove,___ And as I
-witch-ing shades!___ Each sad-ly smiles at me,___ With each I

dream, My fan-cy turns to Love!___
swore, To love e-ter-nal-ly!___

rit.

(He rolls a cigarette)

Love is like a ci-gar-ette (A ci-gar-ette may last as long.)

pp molto delicato

Rose of the World.

Zoradie.

Lyric by
GLEN MAC DONOUGH.

Music by
VICTOR HERBERT.

In all the Sul-tan's gar-dens are ros-es sweet and rare And some are proud and roy-al And some are soft and rare In all the Sul-tan's gar-dens no rose is bloom-ing now As fra-grant or as ten-der as

hours   that pass and leave me   sad   and lone,   While thee I

mf poco agitato

wait   my dear- est one, my   own,   When I thy

song   at morn-ing, noon   or night   hear,   For thee I

long   Ah! would that thou   wert near   Thy song di-

OSCAR HAMMERSTEIN PRESENTS

NAUGHTY MARIETTA

A COMIC OPERA
WITH MLLE. EMMA TRENTINI
BOOK & LYRICS BY
RIDA JOHNSON YOUNG
MUSIC BY

VICTOR HERBERT

Theatrical and Music Hall Rights of these Songs are fully protected by Copyright
and MUST NOT be used for public performances without permission.

M. WITMARK & SONS
NEW YORK ~ CHICAGO ~ SAN FRANCISCO ~ LONDON · PARIS

Ah! Sweet Mystery Of Life.

(The Dream Melody.)

Lyric by
RIDA JOHNSON YOUNG.

Music by
VICTOR HERBERT.

love a-lone that rules for aye! For 'tis love and love a-lone, the world is

seek-ing, For 'tis love and love a-lone that can re-pay! 'Tis the

an-swer, 'tis the end and all of liv-ing! For it is love a-lone that rules for

aye!

Dance Of The Marionettes.

DUET.

Marietta and Rudolfo.

Lyric by
RIDA JOHNSON YOUNG.

Music by
VICTOR HERBERT.

RUDOLFO. (Operating Marionettes.)

Tur - na like dat - a Pier-rette, just so, Bow to the la - dy, Sig - nor Pier - rot.

I'm Falling In Love With Some One.

Captain Dick.

Lyric by
RIDA JOHNSON YOUNG.

Music by
VICTOR HERBERT.

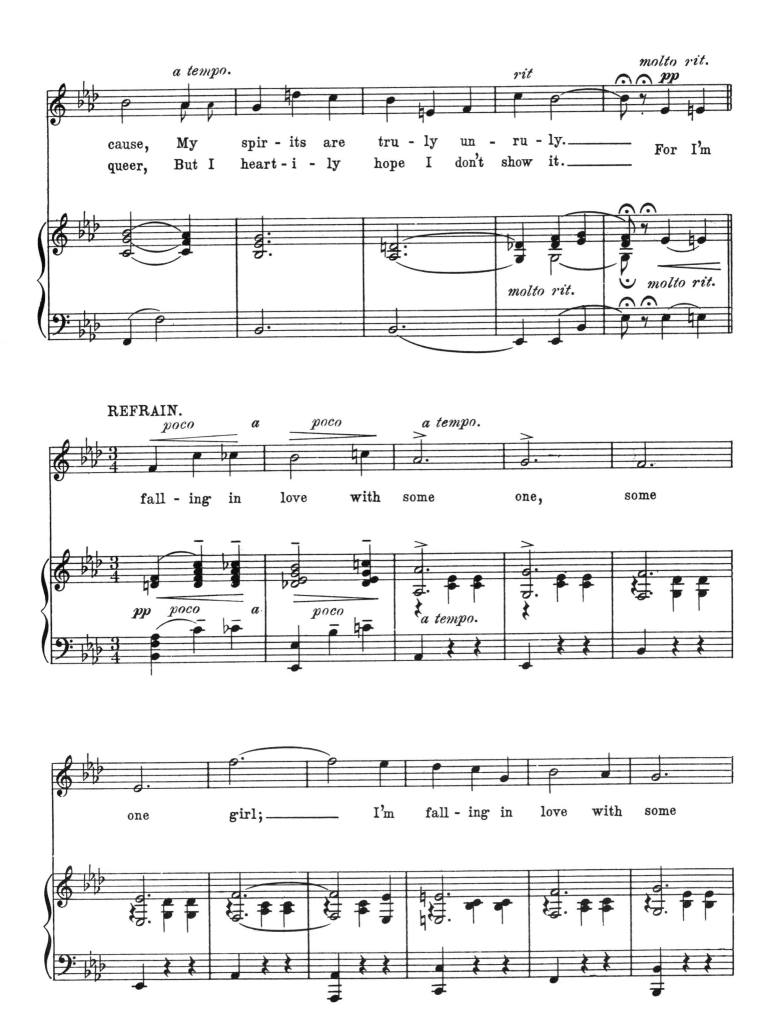

cause, My spir - its are tru - ly un - ru - ly._____ For I'm
queer, But I heart - i - ly hope I don't show it._____

REFRAIN.

fall - ing in love with some one, some
one girl;_____ I'm fall - ing in love with some

Italian Street Song.

Marietta and Chorus.

Lyric by
RIDA JOHNSON YOUNG.

Music by
VICTOR HERBERT.

re - vel - ry___ her sweet re - vel - ry___ The man - do -

li - na's play - ing sweet, the pleas - ant fall of

dan ___ cing feet, Oh! could I re - turn, oh! joy ___ com -

plete, Na - po - li, Na - po - li, Na - po - li!___

Naughty Marietta.

Lyric by
RIDA JOHNSON YOUNG.

Music by
VICTOR HERBERT.

Animato.

Piano.

semplice.   meno.

There are   two   lit - tle maid - ens that   live   in my heart,   And
Come a   time   to the con - vent they   sent   me straight off,   I'm

one   is   so   good,   like___   dis!   She   look   comme ça,   and she
not   fond   of   dat,   not___   me!   I   say   my pray'r,   well most

a tempo.

talk: "La, la!" Like but - ter would melt,— I guess.———— But the
ev - 'ry-where! And bet - ter than gold— I be.———— But the

oth - er lit - tle maid - en, dat's al - - so me, Has a
naught-y Ma - ri - et - ta, dat's al - - so me, Make dat

tem - per so warm, it's— tor - rid!———— So when I am good, I am
con - vent so warm, 'twas— tor - rid!———— 'Cause when she was good, she was

ver - y good in - deed, But when I am bad, I'm hor - rid!

ver - y good in - deed, But when she was bad, she was hor - rid!

REFRAIN. *Molto rubato.*

"Naught - y Ma - ri - et - ta, come be good," says she, "Mais

p a tempo rubato.

non,"—— say me;——— Naught - y Ma - ri - et - ta, but you

p colla voce. *a tempo.*

'Neath The Southern Moon.

Adah.

Lyric by
RIDA JOHNSON YOUNG.

Music by
VICTOR HERBERT.

hearts, you rule, you rule for - ev - er, Queen of hearts, whose pow'r shall ev - er

grow.___ No, no, no, no! I'll look—I'll see no fur - ther!_____ For if 'tis

lost, I can - not, dare not know.

Piu lento, molto appassionato.

'Neath the South - ern moon, 'Oh, love so warm and ten - der!

By the South - ern sea, Oh, love so warm and free!

'Neath the spread - ing shade Of palms, in sweet sur - ren - der,

While the breez - es per - fume la - den drift from sea.

In the South - land, where the scent of the Mag - no - lias

steep the soul in dreams Of long-ing ec - sta - sy,

Where the trop - ics blooms so rare, Breathe their lan - guor on the air.

Let me dream and love and live for thee! For thee!

Tramp! Tramp! Tramp!

Lyric by
RIDA JOHNSON YOUNG

Music by
VICTOR HERBERT

Allegro marcato

We've hunt - ed the wolf in the for - est, We've
We've ranged o'er the North in the win - ter, We've

raid - ed the pi - rates at sea,_____ We have no in - den - ture, we're
an - swered the call of the wild,_____ We heard the wolf call - ing when

out for ad - ven - ture, As an - y one plain - ly can see._____ We've
night-time was fall - ing, And burn-ing logs high - er we piled._____ We've

smoked the peace pipe with the Natch - es, We've
fought for our scalps with the In - dians, We've

fought with the Sioux, wild and free._____ We've laughed at all dan-gers, We're
wa - ded in blood to the knee._____ We've laughed at all dan-gers, We're

known as the Ran-gers: Har-ry Blake, my good com-rades, with me.
known as the Ran-gers: Har-ry Blake, my good com-rades, with me.

REFRAIN *Marziale*

Tramp, tramp, tramp a - long the high - way,

Tramp, tramp, tramp, the road is free;

Bla - zing trails a - long the

by - way,

Cou - riers de Bois____ are we.

Tramp, tramp, tramp, now clear the road way;

Room, room, room, the world is free! _____ We're
Plant - ers and Ca - nucks; Vir - gin - ians and Kain - tucks, Cap - tain
Dick's own In - fan - try, Cap - tain Dick's own In - fan -
try! _____ Dick's own In - fan - try. _____

Natoma

An Opera in Three Acts

The Book by JOSEPH D. REDDING

The Music by

VICTOR HERBERT

Published Separately

IN MY DREAMS (*Paul*) Act I
  Tenor in D♭   Baritone in B♭

SERENADE. When the Sunlight Dies. (*Alvarado*) Act I
  Baritone

VAQUERO'S SONG. Who Dares the Bronco Wild Defy? (*Pico*) Act II
  Tenor in E min.   Baritone in D min.

I LIST THE TRILL IN GOLDEN THROAT. (*Barbara*) Act II
  Soprano in F   Mezzo-Soprano in D

BEWARE OF THE HAWK, MY BABY. Indian Lullaby. (*Natoma*) Act III
  Soprano

FOUR DANCES. Arranged for Piano Solo

  1. HABANERA
  2. MINUET
  3. PAÑUELO
  4. DAGGER DANCE

PRELUDE TO ACT III. Arranged for Piano Solo

G. SCHIRMER, INC., NEW YORK

Dagger Dance

From the opera "Natoma"

Victor Herbert

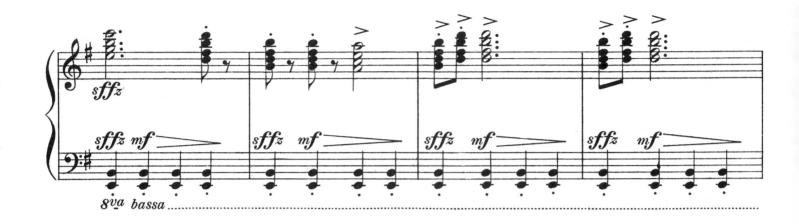

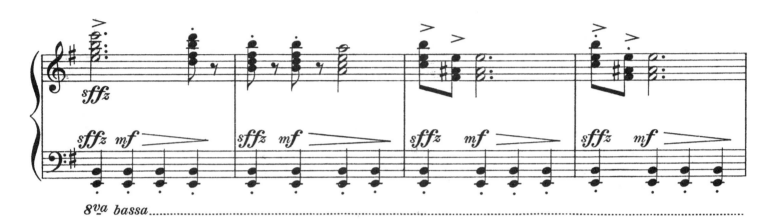

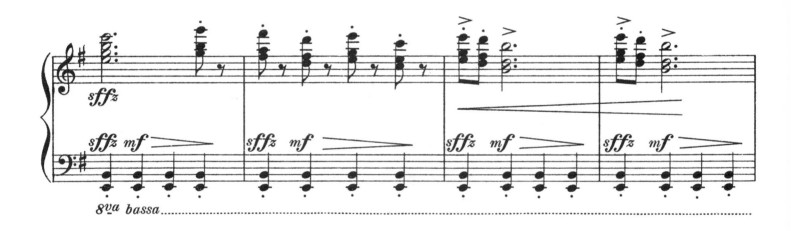

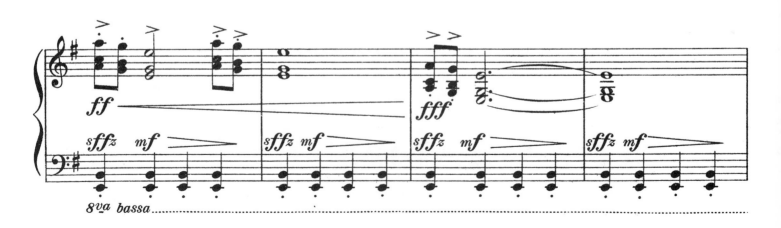

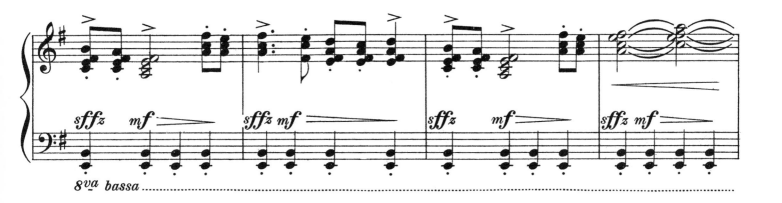

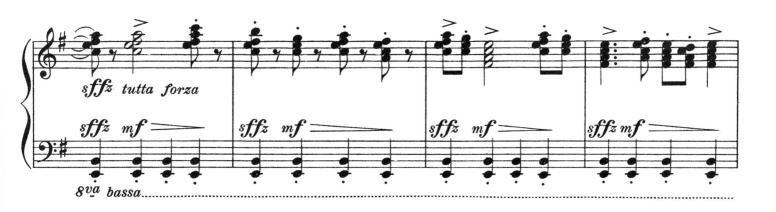

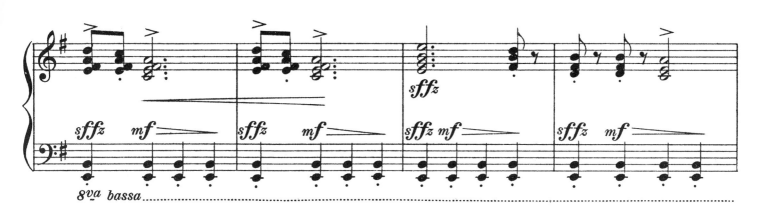

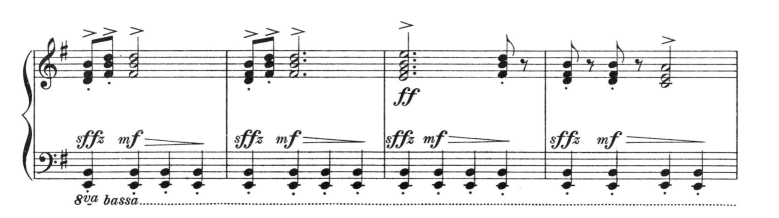

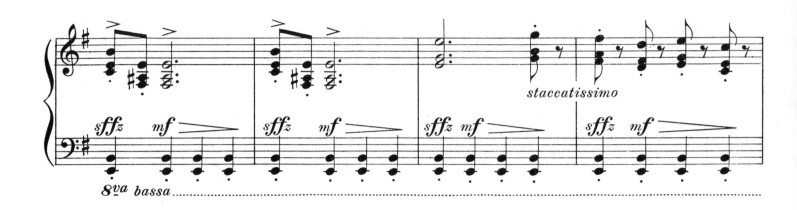

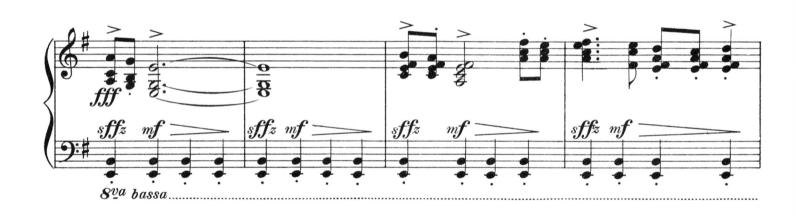

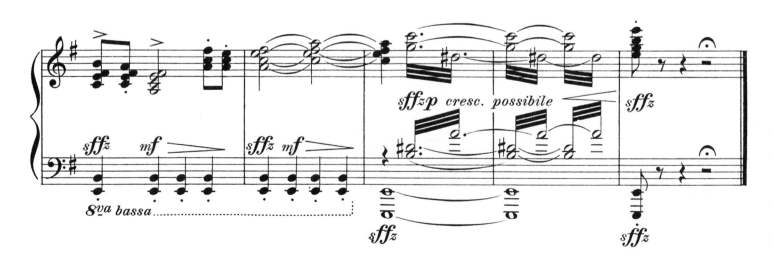

TO THE LAND OF MY OWN ROMANCE

JOSEPH M. GAITES·

PRESENTS

THE ENCHANTRESS

AN OPERA COMIQUE

WITH

KITTY GORDON

BOOK AND LYRICS BY FRED DE GRESAC & HARRY B SMITH

MUSIC BY

VICTOR HERBERT

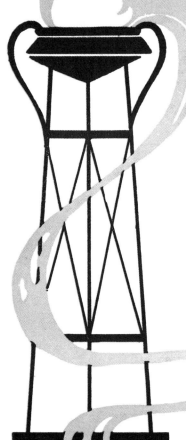

ALL YOUR OWN AM I (Champagne Song)	.	60
ART IS CALLING FOR ME		
(I Want to be a Prima Donna)		60
COME LITTLE FISHES . . .	.	60
DREAMING PRINCESS (Madrigal) . .	.	75
IF YOU CAN'T BE AS HAPPY AS YOU'D LIKE		
TO BE--BE JUST AS HAPPY AS YOU CAN		60
TO THE LAND OF MY OWN ROMANCE (Dream Song)		60
I'VE BEEN LOOKING FOR THE PERFECT MAN		60
LAST LITTLE GIRL IS YOU, THE . .	.	60
ONE WORD FROM YOU (Duet) . .	.	60
ROSE LUCKY ROSE	.	60
THAT NAUGHTY LITTLE SONG . . .	.	60
THEY ALL LOOK GOOD WHEN THEY'RE FAR AWAY		60
WHEN THE RIGHT MAN SINGS "TRA LA"	.	60

INSTRUMENTAL

WALTZES	. .	75	SELECTION .	. 1.00
SCORE	. . . .			. 2.50

M WITMARK & SONS

NEW YORK ~ CHICAGO ~ SAN FRANCISCO ~ LONDON ~ PARIS

DE TAKACS

To The Land Of My Own Romance.
(I Have A Dream By Night, By Day.)

Lyric by
HARRY B. SMITH.

Music by
VICTOR HERBERT.

Framed in the glare of an
Car - men the Gyp - sy with

arch bright and gold - en, A fig - ure of fan - cy am I;
love and hate flow - ing, The sor - row of Mig - non so sweet.

Just like the slum - ber - ing Prin - cess in old - en Ro -
El - sa who sighed her Knight's name to be know - ing Then

man - ces, my life pass - es by. _____ Play - ing at pas - sion, in
brief joys of poor Mar - gue - rite. _____ Love - lorn I - sol - de and

po - e - try feign - ing, Striv - ing and liv - ing for art.
Thä - is en - tranc - ing. Sing them for fame and for pelf.

Men say "La Di - va" is peer - less - ly reign - ing, But what has be - come of
Liv - ing in her - o - ine's love and ro - manc - ing, But where am I all this

molto marcato.

me— who knows? And what has be-come of my   heart?_____

time— who knows? And what has be-come of my - self?_____

REFRAIN. *Valse Lente.*

I have a dream by night, by day._____   'Tis not of

lau - rels___ fair._____   Dream of a song that's still un-

Presented by WERBA & LUESCHER
with CHRISTIE MACDONALD in the cast

SWEETHEARTS

Comic Opera in Two Acts

BOOK BY HARRY B. SMITH & FRED. DE GRESSAC
LYRICS BY ROBERT B. SMITH

Music By
VICTOR HERBERT

VOCAL SCORE 2.00 *net*

PUBLISHED SEPARATELY

FOR VOICE AND PIANO

Sweethearts. (Sylvia) High

Every Lover must Meet his Fate. (Prince) High (or Medium)

Mother Goose. (Sylvia) High (or Medium)

The Cricket on the Hearth. (Sylvia) High (or Medium)

The Ivy and the Oak. (Sylvia) High

There is Magic in a Smile. (Liane) High

Jeannette and Her Little Wooden Shoes. (Liane) High (or Medium)

Each, 50 cents

FOR VIOLIN AND PIANO
Entr'acte   50 cents

NEW YORK : G. SCHIRMER
BOSTON : THE BOSTON MUSIC CO.
LONDON : SCHOTT & CO.

Angelus
Duet

Lyrics by
Robert B. Smith

From the Comic Opera
"Sweethearts" by
Victor Herbert

Now on the air a sol-emn si-lence falls And holds me in its spell;

149

153

Every Lover Must Meet His Fate

Lyrics by
Robert B. Smith

From the Comic Opera
"Sweethearts," by
Victor Herbert

Più meno ... più rit. ... Molto meno

Still, when I am a-lone,___ For love do I sigh.___

molto sentito

But ev-'ry lov-er Must meet his fate,___ So for that hour___ My heart will

molto espressivo

wait.___ As all sur-ren-der— (Who would de-fy?)___ To tempt-ing

kiss-es ten-der, So will I,___ will I!

Jeannette and Her Little Wooden Shoes

From the Comic Opera
"Sweethearts" by
Victor Herbert

Lyrics by
Robert B. Smith

plen - ty of suit - ors, had on - ly to
cold win - ter night, when the town was a -

choose: And be - ing a Dutch girl, she wore wood - en
sleep, The two stole a - way, though the snow was quite

shoes. When she stole out at night all the town knew the
deep.— The King cried: "Pur - sue them! Which way did they

news, When they heard the pit - pat - ter of her wood - en
go?" The guards and the court - iers they ran to and

shoes.___ Then the lads, half a-sleep, oh how jeal-ous they'd
fro;___ And he might be pur-su-ing those two lov-ers

get, And they'd say to them-selves, "Who is out with Jean-nette?"
yet, But those wood-en shoe-tracks in the snow spell'd Jean-nette!

Clip clop clop! Clip clop clop! O-ver the tiles. Her
Clip clop clop! Clip clop clop! There in the snow Her

feet were pe-tite, But you heard her for miles,___ With her
feet so pe-tite, Showed them which way to go,___ With her

pit - ter, pit - ter, pat - ter, clip clop clop, gos - sip pur - sues The
pit - ter, pit - ter, pat - ter, clip clop clop, they found the clues, And Jean -

se - crets be - trayed by Jean - nette's wood - en shoes!
nette lost her Prince through the prints of her shoes!

Wooden-shoe Dance

D.C.

Pretty as a Picture

Lyrics by
Robert B. Smith

From the Comic Opera
"Sweethearts" by
Victor Herbert

161

won - der all the men declare: "She's pret-ty as a pic-ture,

Bloom-ing as a rose, Grace in ev - ry move - ment, Charm in ev - ry

pose." Ha! ha! O clev-er lit - tle wo-man, We all un-der-stand That

Na- ture can - not make you What you can do by hand

Sweethearts

Lyrics by
Robert B. Smith

From the Comic Opera
"Sweethearts," by
Victor Herbert

If you ask where love is found, The sort of love that's fond and true, I will bid you look a-round; It may be ver-y near to you.

Some-times love is ver-y try-ing, But you real-ly must not mind it;

If it comes not to your sigh-ing, There is al-ways one place you may find it;

Seek the dwell-ing of two hap-py sweet-hearts, You will find it there!

Sweet-hearts make love their ver-y own, Sweet-hearts can live on love a-lone,

For them the eyes where love-light lies O-pen the gates to Par-a-dise! All oth-er

love is doomed to fade, It is like sun-shine veiled in shade, Such joys of

life as love im-parts Are all of them yours, sweet - hearts!